I Know the Rules!

I AM KIND TO OTHERS!

By Bray Jacobson

Gareth Stevens
PUBLISHING

Please visit our website, www.garethstevens.com. For a free color catalog of all our high-quality books, call toll free 1-800-542-2595 or fax 1-877-542-2596.

Library of Congress Cataloging-in-Publication Data

Names: Jacobson, Bray, author.
Title: I am kind to others! / Bray Jacobson.
Description: Buffalo, New York : Gareth Stevens Publishing, [2024] | Series: I know the rules! | Includes index.
Identifiers: LCCN 2022051445 (print) | LCCN 2022051446 (ebook) | ISBN 9781538286531 (library binding) | ISBN 9781538286524 (paperback) | ISBN 9781538286548 (ebook)
Subjects: LCSH: Kindness–Juvenile literature.
Classification: LCC BJ1533.K5 J33 2024 (print) | LCC BJ1533.K5 (ebook) | DDC 177/.7–dc23/eng/20230111
LC record available at https://lccn.loc.gov/2022051445
LC ebook record available at https://lccn.loc.gov/2022051446

Published in 2024 by
Gareth Stevens Publishing
2544 Clinton Street
Buffalo, NY 14224

Copyright © 2024 Gareth Stevens Publishing

Designer: Claire Wrazin
Editor: Kristen Nelson

Photo credits: Cover, p. 1 Africa Studio/Shutterstock.com; p. 5 Monkey Business Images/Shutterstock.com; p. 7 Drazen Zigic/Shutterstock.com; p. 9 Pixel-Shot/Shutterstock.com; p. 11 fizkes/Shutterstock.com; p. 13 Ermolaev Alexander/Shutterstock.com; p. 13 (inset) Robert Kneschke/Shutterstock.com; pp. 15, 24 (hug) Svitlana Bezuhlova/Shutterstock.com; p. 17 Jaromir Chalabala/Shutterstock.com; p. 19 VP Photo Studio/Shutterstock.com; p. 21 Maria Evseyeva/Shutterstock.com; p. 23 WiP-Studio/Shutterstock.com; p. 24 (card) A StockStudio/Shutterstock.com

All rights reserved. No part of this book may be reproduced in any form without permission in writing from the publisher, except by a reviewer.

Printed in the United States of America

CPSIA compliance information: Batch #CSGS24: For further information contact Gareth Stevens, at 1-800-542-2595.

Contents

What Is Kindness? 4

Kind Words 6

Kind Actions 12

Your Turn! 22

Words to Know 24

Index. 24

I am kind to others!
I use kind words.
I do kind actions.

Kumail uses kind words.
He wants more bread.
He says, "please."

Paul gets a gift.
He says, "Thank you."

Farah feels upset.
She does not yell.
She says what is wrong.

What are kind actions?

Zara sees a sad friend.
She gives them a hug.

Mitchell thinks
of his grandma.
He sends her a card.

Jocelyn sees Peter fall.
She helps him up.

Tara's mom made lunch.
Tara cleans up after!

How can you be kind
to others?

Words to Know

card   hug

Index

clean up, 20   please, 6
hug, 14   thank you, 8